TEACHING ENGL

Publication Details

Teaching English: A Practitioner's Guide by Gregory Macur

Published by Macur Ed Series

Online Publication

www.gregorymacur.com

Copyright ©2020 Gregory Macur

All rights reserved. No portion of this book may be reproduced in any form without permission from the publisher, except as permitted by copyright law. For permissions contact: gregoryteaches@gmail.com

Cover by Macur Ed Series

ISBN: 978-1-3999-2485-6

Printed in United Kingdom

2nd Edition

Contents Page

Contents Page..3
Who is Gregory Macur? 7
Important To Know...7
Why you should read this book..8
Why I wrote this book..9
Introduction..11
Greg's Must Know 50 word How-Tos...13
    Possible Teaching Aids 16
    A Simple Speaking Lesson Structure - From Beginning To End 17
    A Simple Reading Lesson Structure - From Beginning To End 19
    A Simple Writing Lesson Structure - From Beginning To End 21
    A Simple Listening Lesson Structure - From Beginning To End......... 23
Section 1 Kindergarten..**25**
Speaking...**26**
    Fun Drill...27
    High And Low Drill 28
    Blow It Up Drill 29
    Pass And Say Drill 30
    Rotisserie 31
    Teacher Zombie...32
    Sing Along Routines 33
    Sing Along Drills..34
    Speaking Musical Statues..35
    Low Level Role Play 36
    X And O Practice 37
Reading..**38**

- Guessing The Story 39
- Read And Find It Out 40
- Reading Language Drill 41
- Spot The Picture 42
- Finger Following 43
- Is it Good Or Bad 44
- Read And Act 45
- Choral Reading 46
- What Happens Next? 47
- Reading Crafts 48

Writing **49**
- Tracing Worksheet 50
- Trace And Match 51
- Colour The Letter 52
- One Letter Gap Fill 53
- Circle The Word 54
- Listen And Write 55
- Walk And Trace 56
- Dot To Dot Letter Exposure 57
- Look And Write 58
- Free Writing For Kindergarten 59

Listening **60**
- Listen And Colour 61
- Listen And Circle 62
- Listen And Number 63
- Listen And Connect The Letters 64
- Listen And Act 65
- Treasure hunt 66
- Listen And Slap 67

Listen And Trace 68

Move And Stop 69

Section 2 Primary 70

Speaking 71

Find Somebody Who 72

Pair Work Drill 73

Rock Paper Scissors Review 74

Surveys 75

Questionnaire 76

Board Games 77

Big Dice Drill 78

Snowball Fight 79

Tell 5 Friends 80

Ladder Climb 81

Reading 82

Read And Answer 83

Running Dictation 84

Face Away Reading 85

Whole Text Gap fill 86

1 Minute Skim 87

Scanning 88

Surveying 89

Speed Read 90

Read And Summarise 91

Team Choral Reading 92

Writing 93

Write A Short Story 94

Finish the story 95

Add The Adjectives/Adverbs 96

- Write An Opinion Piece 97
- Free Writing For Primary 98
- One Sentence Each 99
- Write A Letter (formal or informal) 100
- Opposites... 101
- Condensation... 102
- Poetry and Rhyming... 103

Listening..**104**
- Listen And Answer 105
- Listen And Sort... 106
- Listen For Gist Group Poster... 107
- Listen And Discuss.. 108
- Listen And Order... 109
- Who Said It?... 110
- Descriptive Selection... 111
- Listen And Create.. 112
- Dictogloss 113
- Listen And Draw.. 114

What now? **115**
Bonus Activities...**116**
Acronyms & Definitions..**116**
Bibliography...**118**

Who is Gregory Macur?

Gregory Macur is a working teacher, school leader, educational researcher, teacher trainer and educational author. He is currently completing his PhD and developing a body of educational contributions. His other works include: "Teaching Online for Kindergarten and Primary Teachers" published by Routledge.

Important To Know

The activities in this book are split into Kindergarten and Primary. **This does not mean the activities are only for those age groups.** Great teachers take ideas from all areas; some Kindergarten activities are great for Primary learners and vice versa. It is up to the teacher to adapt and apply these activities in ways that suit them and their learners. Also, as the author of this book, I am not instructing teachers to go and do these activities. I am simply sharing my experience and what research has indicated to be good practice.

My favourite activities in each section are tagged with two stars, like this: My favourite ★ ★.

Why you should read this book

This book will benefit your students. The activities and ideas in here are ones that I have seen work time and time again. Beyond that, this book has been combed over by qualified and experienced professionals who added value in their feedback each time.

This book will benefit you! No more hours of trying to figure out a way to get the kids communicating; no more confusion on how to motivate students to write; no more reading comprehension problems & no more repetitive listening activities. It is all here, ready for you to use!

It is practical – not theoretical

The ideas in here are for you to use; not for you to read about and do nothing with. You can open this book to any page and take practical value (I challenge you.) It is not a bulky text book, nor is it filled with unnecessary jargon (there is a short acronyms and definitions section on page 104 just in case.) Use it well and improve your practice starting today.

Everything is tried and tested

The activities are ones that have worked well for hundreds of teachers. Not only this, the book is laid out in the simplest and most digestible way possible – this makes its use and application particularly easy.

It was written for you and your students

Each activity tells you interaction patterns; how to increase and decrease difficulty; estimated duration and what materials (if any) you need.

There are lesson structures, key ideas and tools you can use... It truly is a practitioner's guide.

Why I wrote this book

I believe in sharing ideas; I believe in raising education standards worldwide; I believe in my job; I believe in self-improvement; I believe in communicating in the simplest way possible, not dancing around jargon needlessly; I believe in the value of language learning, and I believe the meaning of life is found in improvement and focus on something productive and helpful (Macur, 2020).

I have spent years trying different activities; I still haven't got it right. I have, however, found the ones that have time and time again worked very well, got students to meet learning objectives and are transferable across topics.

Early in my career, I noticed that teachers often struggled with activity ideas (I was one of them). This filled me with desire to deeply understand the different ways you can engage students in a learning space. Years later, whilst I was mentoring co-teachers, I learnt that I was not the only one with this desire.

I decided to write this book whilst sitting in the staff room listening to some of my peers who were struggling with ideas for their lessons. I regularly shared my ideas with them and had become known for doing so. I opened my phone and drew a picture in my notes (see the last few pages of the book). That was that.

I have created training courses for teachers to improve their abilities to work with EFL, ESL and EAL learners. Another big drive for me to write this book was as a gift to those who pass my courses: a simple gesture of my gratitude to them for being dedicated to reflect and improve as teachers. Not only to them, but also to you; if you are reading my book you are the kind of teacher who seeks knowledge, reflection and improvement. I would like to extend my gratitude for your approach to education and yourself.

Introduction

Engaging students in a foreign language can prove to be extremely difficult if the activities, games and lessons are boring (Gao, 2010). One of the main causes of misbehaviour in classrooms is boredom (Altinel, 2006). A lack of diverse and engaging activities can lead to this kind of boredom (Dumančić, 2018). The best way to combat problems like boredom in a classroom you ask? PPPPP "Proper Planning Prevents Poor Performance." The truest phrases carry their weight globally; this is one of them. This book is in essence, the best activities and approaches to teaching Kindergarten & Primary learners a teacher can come up with over years of reflection (that is how long it took me to run through 1000s of activities and create this guide)

"How do you plan towards a great lesson? What even is a lesson?"

A lesson is, in effect, a series of activities that are done to meet learning objectives. Great lessons therefore, are a series of great activities that are done to meet learning objectives. This book gives you those activities.

"What are learning objectives?"

Learning objectives are what teachers want the students to learn. Lessons and activities are formulated around lesson objectives; these are attached to the curriculum and should be implemented cumulatively. This book provides logical structures for you.

"So, what are great activities?"

Great activities are usable in many different ways; they are engaging; fun wherever possible; they push students; they are safe; they are easily differentiated so that weak students can take part; they meet learning objectives and are SMART (Specific, Measurable, Achievable, Relevant, Time-constrained). Great activities can offer students some opportunity to compete and engage in team/group-based learning; they offer students an opportunity to explore and/or figure things out autonomously. Only sometimes should activities be teacher-centred or led; let them lead themselves! Facilitate.

Structure of this book

This book has been written in the most digestible and simply understandable way. Wherever possible, activities are presented in a light-hearted and entertaining manner. The book progresses chronologically from the age 2 all the way up to High School.

The sections progress activities logically through what would be a lesson structure; as such, the activities at the start of the section are easier and are more focussed on accuracy and remembering; as the section moves on, the activities begin to be more fluency and mastery focussed.

For new teachers

This book is intended to be the foundation of your own activity bank; you should copy the activities you like best down in your own folder, book or online drive; then begin to add your own. It will expose you to the ideas such as student interaction patterns and learning styles. Once you are familiar with the classroom and using deeply varied activities to meet lesson objectives, you can begin to make changes that suit the teaching style that you are developing

For experienced teachers

This book is intended to be a source from which to add to your activity bank. As such, taking ideas from here and adapting them is encouraged strongly. Trying out different things that you may not normally do can expose your students to a bit of variety in the classroom. "The best teachers never stop learning."

From my experience

There is no one activity that fits all. The activities I list in this book are flexible and should be adapted to meet your lesson objectives and the needs of your students.

People with humility who care about their students' development, (as well as their own personal development), make the best teachers. They are the kind of people I could happily sit down and try to learn something from.

Greg's Must Know 50 word How-Tos

Drill effectively
Drilling needs to be fun and engaging. It is typically done to improve students' accuracy and student errors should be corrected immediately. Rewarding students who participate and offering praise is a must. Try to turn drilling into competitive team games; this is key (Richards & Rodgers, 2014).

Motivate the class
Motivating the class is almost always connected to positive reinforcement. Use engaging and relatable activities and make sure reward systems are in place (when necessary). Mix up activities and ensure the learning environment is dynamic. Competitive activities tend to work very well (Reid, 2007).

Give instructions and model an activity
Giving instructions is so important. The best way is to follow a KISS system. Keep It Simple for Students. Avoid unnecessary words and make sure your directions are clear (use concise teacher talk). Remember, demonstration and activity modelling is always your best option (Harmer, 2008).

Monitor an activity
When monitoring an activity, teachers should be looking for mistakes, errors, misconceptions and any problems that may arise. Whether these errors are corrected immediately or later on depends on the activity (improving accuracy = immediate error correction, improving fluency = delayed error correction) (Rahimi & Dastjerdi, 2012). Typically, teachers need to motivate students with praise and positive reinforcement too.

Encourage student to student interaction
Encouraging student to student interaction is something that teachers must be great at. It can be done by setting group/pair work. Giving students more independence and letting them take control of activities can also help (Galton & Williamson, 2003).

Make a reward system
Reward systems play a huge role in driving students to do work. Reward systems should be clear and offer prizes. Wherever possible they should be entertaining and relevant to the lesson content (Dornyei & Kubanyiova, 2014).

Blending and Segmenting

	Blending	**Segmenting**
Definition	Blending in phonics, is when the teacher sounds out the sounds or syllables of a word and slowly blends them together (Pang, Bernhardt, & Kamil, 2003).	Segmenting in phonics, is when the teacher says a word, has the class repeat it, and then slowly breaks it down into its individual sounds or syllables (Pang, Bernhardt, & Kamil, 2003).
Example	b, a, t - ba, t - bat f, a, s, t, er fa, s, ter fas, ter faster	bat - ba, t - b, a, t faster fas, ter fa, s, ter f, a, s, t, er
How we use it	Introduce the word letter by letter (as seen above.) Sound out each letter individually. Slowly blend the sounds together. This is useful when teaching reading too.	Introduce the word as a whole (as seen above.) Have the class repeat it. Slowly deconstruct the word into its individual sounds or syllables. This is useful when teaching reading too.

Back chaining

Back chaining is an effective way of helping students with sound and word formation. It is where you start by saying only the ending sound, then the last two sounds, then the last three sounds and finally, the whole word (British Council).

Example: "ng". "ing". "aining". "chaining". ackchaining". "Backchaining".

This allows students to see how you are saying each part individually. You can also apply this methodology to connected speech (how we connect certain word when we speak) (British Council).

Possible Teaching Aids

This is a short list of resources that you can draw upon for your lessons. This is not a dictation. It is a collection of things that have brought value to my lessons and school environment.

Flashcards – Great for games and activities.

Realia – Real life objects – great for creating context.

The internet – Limitless resources at a teacher's disposal.

The board – Use it well, clear and well laid out.

Worksheets – Great for assessing students throughout a lesson.

Videos – Great for engaging students and giving context.

Music – Even better if the music is what the students like.

Board games – Great for making learning fun.

TPR – total physical response (the actions you make to help give meaning to words).

Body language – Even how you stand matters.

Cues and Gestures – Guiding students with these is key.

Co-workers – They will know something you don't... So ASK!

Little teacher – Students love to take control, let them.

The class – Let them feed each other knowledge.

Parents – Get them on board, they really do tend to care.

The school – A body of knowledge and experience, let them help you.

This list can go on as long as you want. BE CREATIVE!

A Simple Speaking Lesson Structure - From Beginning To End

Warmer - Quick activity to review previous content and set the tone for the lesson.

Introduction - Introduce yourself to the students, check attendance and write lesson objectives on the board.

Presentation

Presentation refers to the initial part of the lesson where the target language (the language intended to be taught) is introduced/presented to the students (Maftoon & Sarem, 2015). When introducing new language, teachers should see what students already know. This can be done by eliciting words from stronger students using pictures or actions.

Presentation of new language needs to be clear and repetition is hugely important during this stage. To keep students focused, teachers should find entertaining ways of drilling (Awaluddin, 2013). One easy way to do this is to create team-based competitions in which students are required to repeat the words.

Practice

This is where students are given the opportunities to practice the target language through a small series of activities (Maftoon & Sarem, 2015). These activities should progress from highly controlled (giving little room for error or creativity), to less-controlled as they master the language.

During this stage, error correction is highly important. You can encourage students to assist each other and you should be monitoring constantly, offering more guidance to weak students.

Production

This is the lesson stage, in which students use the language they have learnt in a flexible way with little or no control. It is more common to have freer practices here (Maftoon & Sarem, 2015).

The students have the opportunity to apply the new language in relatable ways; you can use local pop culture to spark interest. For example, if you had taught hobbies, for younger kids in Asia, the question could be, "what are Doraemon's hobbies?" Group work is a good idea here, as strong students can support weaker students in the group. To incentivise, teachers should offer prizes for teams that work well.

Closing routines - These are what you normally do to close off your lesson. Every teacher should have them: tidy up song, plenary to check what students have learnt etc.

A Simple Reading Lesson Structure - From Beginning To End

Warmer - Quick activity to review previous content and set the tone for the lesson.

Introduction - Introduce yourself to the students, check attendance and write lesson objectives on the board.

Pre-reading

Pre-reading takes place before the reading has begun. During this stage, you are really trying to emphasise the context and activate existing schemata. Pre-reading activities get students excited and interested in what they are about to read; this is key in motivating them to do so. Good activities for this stage are: discussions, pictionary, guessing from pictures/words/sentences and much more. Teachers should make these student-centred (Saricoban, 2002).

While-reading

"While-reading activities" take place once students have started reading the text, but not after it has been finished. During the while reading stage of a lesson, students are able to confirm predictions, gather information and organise information (Saricoban, 2002).

Good activities that can keep the students focussed include, underline topics or word types, skim the text for the key theme, read a paragraph and then discuss it with a partner, and much more. These kinds of activities help students retain information and can stage the reading in a way that everybody can keep up.

Post-reading

Post-reading activities are set after the reading has taken place. They are used to further students' understanding and comprehension of a text. They also give the reading some further purpose. Post-reading activities provide students a chance to analyse and consider what they have read.

Good post-reading activities include, quiz your classmates, creative discussions, creative writing and much more. These are a good opportunity for student to student interactions. These kinds of activities push students a little bit harder and give them opportunity to develop many skills. They also activate high order thinking skills like analysis and evaluation (this leads students to content mastery).

Closing routines - These are what you normally do to close off your lesson. Every teacher should have them: tidy up song, plenary to check what students have learnt etc.

A Simple Writing Lesson Structure - From Beginning To End

Warmer - Quick activity to review previous content and set the tone for the lesson.

Introduction - Introduce yourself to the students, check attendance and write lesson objectives on the board.

Generating ideas

During this stage, students are encouraged to begin to create ideas (you can provide authentic materials to facilitate this). One purpose of this stage is to spark student interest and see what they already know (Hyland, 2019).

Focussing ideas

During this stage, students are encouraged to figure out what ideas they are going to focus on. This will be based on the ideas that were generated in the first stage (Hyland, 2019).

Organising ideas

During this stage, students are encouraged to organise these ideas into a logical order. This is an integral part of giving their piece of writing flow and ensuring it makes sense (Hyland, 2019).

Writing

During this stage, students can write up their text. You should be monitoring them and providing inspiration and guidance where necessary (Hyland, 2019).

Peer-evaluation

During this stage, students evaluate each other's work. Peer-evaluation is a key part of learning and should not be skipped (Double, McGrane, & Hopfenbeck, 2020).

Reviewing

During this stage, students review their own work, finding areas they think are good and areas they think could be improved.

Conclusion

During this stage, students can come to a conclusion about their piece of writing or the writing task in general. This can be done as a class or individually: it depends on the learning objectives of the lesson.

Closing routines - These are what you normally do to close off your lesson. Every teacher should have them: tidy up song, plenary to check what students have learnt etc.

A Simple Listening Lesson Structure - From Beginning To End

Warmer - Quick activity to review previous content and set the tone for the lesson.

Introduction - Introduce yourself to the students, check attendance and write lesson objectives on the board.

Pre-listening

Pre-listening activities typically involve some predicting and guessing. You can:

1. Show students the title of the track and they must make predictions about it.
2. Ask them a question that will set the context.
3. Introduce the characters and let them make predictions about them.
4. Tell them the first line and have them guess what comes next.

Pre-listening activities may motivate students and encourage them to listen more intently (Brown, 2018).

While-listening

While-listening activities are designed to keep students focussed during the listening. You can set simple questions that follow the structure of the track; you can pause the track and ask whole class questions; you can set multiple-choice questions; ask students to identify themes; ask students to figure out who did what, and much more (Brown, 2018).

Post-listening

First of all, reassure students and have the class guide answers together; this is an effective way to help weaker students. Refer back to the pre-listening activities and confirm the predictions and guesses. Refer back to the "during listening" activity and check answers/have discussions (Brown, 2018). You can add extensions where students must write the next paragraph and read it to a friend. Highlight any new vocabulary or phrases that are useful for the students to know, and have them apply them to their own lives.

Closing routines - These are what you normally do to close off your lesson. Every teacher should have them: tidy up song, plenary to check what students have learnt etc.

Section 1 Kindergarten

Kindergarten students are lively and explorative, they usually seek the teacher's approval and as such, it can be very easy to motivate them. Classroom management can be difficult but not if the activities are great. As teachers, we need to guide these students carefully. We must use concise "Teacher Talk" and graded language: do this right and your students will shine (Macur G. M., 2020)!

Speaking

When I was a student, my teachers always told me to stop talking to my friends. You can do the opposite! A student-to-student interaction goes a very long way in language retention and development (Balser, Grabau, Kniess, & Page, 2017).

When encouraging kindergarten learners to speak, you need to avoid feeding them language; ensure the students are adequately challenged. Elicit the language from the students; push the students to find the language from their memory banks. You will need to drill the language first, to help them with pronunciation and emphasis. This is early on though. Kindergarten learners are often keen to show you and their friends the language they know: let them.

Fun Drill

Instructions

1. Present the vocabulary using flashcards (Use Concept Checking Questions).
2. Elicit the words from stronger students; if no student knows, you can demonstrate how to say them.
3. Draw a happy face and a sad face on the board.
4. Show the students that when you point to the happy face, they must smile and say the word or image on the flashcard using the happy emotion.
5. Show the students that when you point to the sad face, they must frown and say the word or image on the flashcard using the sad emotion.
6. Repeat this process for as long as necessary, provided it is engaging.
7. Reward students who are trying hard and encourage ones who are not.
8. Drilling should be kept as fun as possible, especially with younger learners.

Ages	Interaction patterns	Estimated duration	Make it easier by	Make it harder by	Materials
2 – 5	T – S S – T	7 minutes	Using less flashcards	Using full sentences or more flashcards	Flash cards, marker

High And Low Drill

Instructions

1. Present the vocabulary using flashcards or realia (Use CCQs)
2. Elicit the words from stronger students, if no students know, you can demonstrate how to say them.
3. Demonstrate to the students that, when your hand is held low down your body, they must say the words in a deep voice, and when your hand is held high above your head, they must say the words in a high voice.
4. Repeat this process for as long as necessary provided it is engaging.
5. Reward students who are trying hard and encourage ones who are not.
6. You can make this a game by rewarding the fastest students.

This is a great way to drill language whilst presenting it.

Ages	Interaction patterns	Estimated Duration	Make it easier by	Make it harder by	Materials
2 – 5	T – S S – T	5 minutes	Requiring students to say only one word	Requiring students to produce long sentences	No preparation

Blow It Up Drill

Instructions

1. Present the vocabulary using flashcards (Use CCQs).
2. Elicit the words from stronger students, if no students know, you can demonstrate how to say them.
3. Show the students a balloon.
4. Demonstrate to them that, when you show them a flashcard, they must say the word or sentence repeatedly, as they do, you blow up the balloon.
5. Once the balloon is full, let it go so it flies around the room (students find this hilarious).
6. Repeat this process as long as necessary provided it is engaging.
7. Reward students who are trying hard and encourage ones who are not.

This is a great activity for drilling language in a fun way.

Ages	Interaction patterns	Estimated Duration	Make it easier by	Make it harder by	Materials
2 – 5	T – S S – T	7 minutes	Using less flashcards	Add in an adjective e.g. "big"	Flashcards, a balloon

Pass And Say Drill

Instructions

1. Present the vocabulary using flashcards or realia (Use CCQs).
2. Elicit the words from stronger students, if no students know, you can demonstrate how to say them.
3. Have the students make a circle and sit down.
4. The students will pass the piece of realia or the flashcard around in a circle saying what it is.
5. The students who are not holding the flashcard can ask, "What is it?"
6. Reward students who are trying hard and encourage ones who are not.
7. You can make this a game by timing it and seeing how fast the class can pass it in a full circle, set time goals and allocate rewards to them.

This is an effective way to drill language as a group, perfect for practicing accuracy.

Ages	Interaction patterns	Estimated duration	Make it easier by	Make it harder by	Materials
2 – 5	T – S S – S	5 minutes	Asking the question yourself	Add in an adjective e.g. "big"	Flashcards, realia

Rotisserie

Instructions

1. Lay some flashcards on the floor facing the class.
2. Demonstrate to the students that, one by one they come up, pick a flashcard and ask the class "what is it?"
3. The class responds by saying what it is.
4. You can make it a race and the fastest student or team to answer can gain points.
5. Reward students who are trying hard and encourage ones who are not.

This gives students the opportunity to communicate and present information.

Ages	Interaction patterns	Estimated duration	Make it easier by	Make it harder by	Materials
4 – 5	T – S S – S	5 – 10 minutes	Only requiring students to say one word	Making the question harder e.g. if the topic is food, the question can be "what food do you like?"	Flashcards

Teacher Zombie

Instructions

1. Stand up the students.
2. Show them a flashcard, they must identify it as a group.
3. They can then take 1 step towards you.
4. Repeat this process till you have covered all of the words and the students are close by.
5. Then you can say teacher zombie and the students return to their chairs.
6. Ensure safety rules are clear and there is nothing obstructing students in the way.
7. Do not force students to take part, only those who feel confident and comfortable doing so.

This is a very fun way to drill and practice language with your students. They will be extremely engaged, and will most likely request this game often.

Ages	Interaction Patterns	Estimated duration	Make it easier by	Make it harder by	Materials
3 – 7	T – S S – S	5 – 10 minutes	Only requiring students to say one word	Requiring full sentences from the students	Flashcards

Sing Along Routines

Instructions

1. Develop some simple songs that can be used at certain times of class, e.g.
"Now it's time to tidy up, tidy up, tidy up. Now it's time to tidy up and put our things away".
2. You can create these songs using functional language and teach the students the lyrics.
3. These songs can be sung to develop language abilities, signify key things to the students and can be very entertaining and engaging for students.
4. Reward students who are trying hard and encourage ones who are not.

This is an engaging way to get students moving and speaking – great for routines.

Ages	Interaction Patterns	Estimated duration	Make it easier by	Make it harder by	Materials
2 – 5	Whole class	1 – 2 minutes	Singing only 1 or 2 words	Adding in some questions for the students to answer	None

Sing Along Drills

Instructions

1. Using the lesson content, teachers can create sing along activities for the class.
2. These should be as simple as possible and can be taught to the class bit by bit.
3. Reward students who are trying hard and encourage ones who are not.

E. g. A food lesson where the content is about what you like and don't like, the song could be:
"Hello food. Hello friends. What food do you like?"
"I like chicken and peas"
"I don't like frogs or bugs"
"No, no, no I don't like frogs or bugs"

Ages	Interaction patterns	Estimated duration	Make it easier by	Make it harder by	Materials
2 – 5	Whole class	10 -15 minutes	Using only 1 or 2 words	Making the song longer	None (maybe flashcards to demo the song

Speaking Musical Statues

Instructions

1. Demonstrate to the students that when the music is playing, they dance or do an action that you tell them.
2. When the music stops they must all stop.
3. Show them a flashcard and they must say what it is.
4. Reward students who are trying hard and encourage ones who are not.
5. You can make this a game by having students who move when the music stops sit down.

This is a fun way to get students moving and using language at the same time.

Ages	Interaction patterns	Estimated duration	Make it easier by	Make it harder by	Materials
3 – 5	T – S S – T	5 – 10 minutes	Requiring students to say only 1 word	Having students say longer more complicated sentences	Something to play music, flashcards

Low Level Role Play

Instructions

1. Demonstrate a role play to the students (using flashcards and visual aids).
2. If the lesson objective is to improve the students' ability to express what they like, the role play could simply be.

A – Hi, what's your name? B – My name is _____, and you?

A – My name is _____. What do you like? B – I like _____. What do you like?

A – Nice to meet you, goodbye. B – Nice to meet you, goodbye.

3. Once the role play has been demonstrated and practiced as a whole class, have two strong students attempt it in front of the class.
4. Then encourage students to work in pairs and practice the role play together.
5. Reward students, who are trying hard and encourage ones who are not.

Ages	Interaction patterns	Estimated duration	Make it easier by	Make it harder by	Materials
5	T – S S – T S – S	15 minutes	Shorten the role play to just 1 line each	Add in some adjectives to the sentences	Flashcards, visual cues

X And O Practice

Instructions

1. Demonstrate to students that when they take their turn at XO, they must ask their partner the key question from your lesson.
2. The question can be tailored to any topic
3. Students cannot repeat the same answer twice.
4. Repeat this process as long as necessary provided it is engaging
5. Reward students who are trying hard and encourage ones who are not

This is a great way to have a class practice the language in a fun way without feeling like they are drilling.

Ages	Interaction patterns	Estimated duration	Make it easier by	Make it harder by	Materials
4 – 5	S – S	5 – 10 minutes	Putting images of the food in each square and requiring students to only say the word	Add in an adjective e.g. "big"	XO worksheets with the title tailored to the lesson aim

Reading

Do not actually feed kids books...

I am an adult and I still can struggle to get myself to read, even though I like it! Imagine being a 4 year old who does not understand the symbols you are showing them; now imagine wanting to pick up that ball over there in the corner; now imagine you telling you to read some symbols instead of playing with the ball. Can you see the problem? Reading needs to be fun, you can help students by making it into games or activating their interest. Always try to use relatable texts. A 3-year old does not want a story about politics, the same as you do not want a story about an ice-cream (maybe you do, perhaps I should not assume!). Making your own texts is often a good idea, it shows the students you put time and effort in it, and this will add value in their eyes. Repetition is key here; just make sure you are not tyrannising your kids.

Guessing The Story

Instructions

1. Show the students the book.
2. Ask the students what they can see on the front, point if you need to.
3. Ask the students to say what they think the book is about.
4. Ask specific questions if you need to, "is it a sad book?"
5. Strong classes can do this in pairs, asking each other the questions.
6. Reward students who are trying hard and encourage ones who are not.

This is a great way to prepare students for the reading part of the lesson; they will be more engaged when reading and will feel more involved with the book. Prediction is a big part of reading lessons.

Ages	Interaction patterns	Estimated duration	Make it easier by	Make it harder by	Materials
3 – 5	T – S	5 – 10 minutes	Asking specific and simple questions	Asking open ended and difficult questions	Books

★ ★My favourite

Read And Find It Out

Instructions

1. Show the students the book.
2. Tell them the title and set the context of the reading.
3. Give them a selection of questions or bits of information they must find.

E.g.
"What animals are in the book?"
"Find out who likes bananas"

4. Keep the questions in line with the lesson objectives. This activity will give meaning and purpose to the reading activity the students need to do.
5. Reward students who are trying hard and encourage ones who are not.

This is a great activity to get students to read for purpose.

Ages	Interaction patterns	Estimated duration	Make it easier by	Make it harder by	Materials
5+	T – S S – T	5 minutes	Using simple questions	Using difficult and complex questions	Books, question worksheets

Reading Language Drill

Instructions

1. Before introducing the book, it is often necessary to drill any language that the students may need to know to understand the story.
2. Do this by using flashcards that correlate with the imagery of the book and have the spelling of the words clear underneath the flashcard.
3. When drilling the words, try to break up the word into its individual letters or sounds (segmenting).
4. You can then begin to merge the letters and sounds with the students (blending).
5. Make the drilling fun by using one of the games mentioned in the speaking section.
6. Reward students who are trying hard and encourage ones who are not.

This is a great way to pre expose the students to the sounds and letters they are going to be encountering.

Ages	Interaction patterns	Estimated duration	Make it easier by	Make it harder by	Materials
3 – 5	T – S S – T	5 – 10 minutes	Focussing more on actions and imagery	Focussing more on the spelling	Books, flashcards, spelling flashcards

Spot The Picture

Instructions

1. Model to the students that as you read the book, they must point at the relevant pictures in the book
2. It is important to ensure the students do not have the books until you model the activity, if you give them out first, the students will be distracted when you give your instructions. ICQ the students regularly.
3. Whilst reading, identify students who are on task and doing well, reward them. This will motivate students who are not on task and it will give students who are struggling a model of how to take part

This is a low-level reading activity and is an effective way to check students understand some of the words they are coming across. This is designed for the younger classes or can be used as a pre-curser to reading a book as a class.

Ages	Interaction patterns	Estimated duration	Make it easier by	Make it harder by	Materials
2 – 5	T – S	5 – 10 minutes	Modelling the activity for its duration	Reading faster or having the students try to speak	Books

Finger Following

Instructions

1. Before handing out the books, demonstrate to the students that as the teacher reads, they must follow each word with their fingers
2. Use a strong student to come to the front and model this too, ICQ the students to ensure they understand
3. If there are no strong students, use your TA
4. Hand out the books
5. Reward students who are trying hard and encourage ones who are not

This is a great activity for exposing students to reading and books. It can be easily altered to be made more difficult and can encourage students to recognise letters

Ages	Interaction patterns	Estimated duration	Make it easier by	Make it harder by	Materials
2 – 5	T – S	5 – 10 minutes	Making large print outs of the pages to enable peer to peer observation	Having the students read	Books, page print outs

Is it Good Or Bad

Instructions

1. Whilst reading the book, the teacher should pause and ask the students, "is it good or bad?"
2. Students must respond with whether what has been read is a good thing or a bad thing.
3. Reward students who are participating.
4. This can be made into a game by rewarding students who are faster at answering.

This is a great way to keep students engaged and focused during the reading stage of the lesson. It is a simple question an example of a CCQ.

Ages	Interaction patterns	Estimated duration	Make it easier by	Make it harder by	Materials
2 – 5	T – S S – T	5 – 10 minutes	Modelling answers if students struggle to understand	Requiring the students to read. Ask them Why it is good or bad.	Books

Read And Act

Instructions

1. Demonstrate to the students that, as a class, you will be reading a book.
2. After each sentence is read, everybody stands up and acts out what they have just read.
3. You can read the book and do the actions on your own first, to give the students an idea of what is expected.
4. Whilst reading, motivate students with rewards to take part and join in.
5. Use a book that contains language which the students are familiar with so as to maximise their understanding.

This is an effective way to expose students to a book and convey meaning behind words.

Ages	Interaction patterns	Estimated duration	Make it easier by	Make it harder by	Materials
4 – 5	T – S S – T	5– 10 minutes	Doing the actions with the kids	Projecting the text onto the board and having the kids read	Books, projector (maybe)

Choral Reading

Instructions

1. Show the students the book.
2. Tell them the title and set the context of the reading.
3. Before handing out the book, inform the students that they will be reading the book as a class together.
4. Hand out the books and begin reading.
5. Use lots of CCQs to ensure students are keeping up with the content and its meaning.
6. Reward students who are trying hard and encourage ones who are not.

This is a commonly used way to ensure all students take part in a reading aloud activity. It can encourage students to be able to keep pace when reading and helps weak students by having strong students as models.

Ages	Interaction patterns	Estimated duration	Make it easier by	Make it harder by	Materials
3 – 5	T – S S – S S – T	5 – 10 minutes	Reading first and having the students repeat	Asking students open questions after each sentence	Books

What Happens Next?

Instructions

1. Whilst reading the book, pause at a cliff-hanger moment.
2. Ask the students what they think will happen next.
3. Encourage them to use full sentences and adjectives.
4. Repeat this process a few times.
5. Reward students who are taking part and encourage students who are not.

This is an activity geared towards prediction and keeping students focussed. Throughout the story, students have the opportunity to express themselves and produce language. You can set this as pair work.

Ages	Interaction patterns	Estimated duration	Make it easier by	Make it harder by	Materials
3 – 5	T – S S – T S – S	5 – 10 minutes	Using imagery to elicit answers	Asking more open ended questions	Books

Reading Crafts

Instructions

1. Once the book has been finished, have a short Q and A relating to what happened.
2. The students can then make a craft that relates to the story and its learning objectives.
3. For example, if the book is, "the hungry caterpillar," the students could make a butterfly craft.
4. Upon completion of the craft, the students can present it to their classmates in a way that is in line with learning objectives.
5. Reward students who take part and try hard.

This is a great way to sum up a story with a kindergarten class. It offers them a chance to be creative. If done properly, it can be in line with learning objectives and give an opportunity to present in front of peers.

Ages	Interaction patterns	Estimated duration	Make it easier by	Make it harder by	Materials
3 – 5	T – S S – S S – T	10 – 15 minutes	Preparing materials for students	Incorporating some writing	Crafts materials

Writing

Sometimes reality is different from expectation.

I remember doing handwriting practice in school and thinking "I can already write, this is a waste of my time." You need to make any writing activity you set interesting, meaningful and engaging.

Some of your students have never held a pen before; bear this in mind when you teach them. Just because it is a writing activity, it does not mean students cannot listen, or speak, or move. If anything, at this age you are sharpening the kids' psychomotor skills (Meyers, 1973). Take advantage of your classroom space: the kids will learn more when you do.

Tracing Worksheet

Instructions

1. Create a tracing worksheet that meets the writing goals in the lesson objectives.
2. Demonstrate to the students how to trace the letters or words.
3. Hand out the worksheets.
4. Hand out the pencils.
5. Monitor the students to see that they are following the correct process.
6. Reward students who are trying hard.

This is an effective way to expose younger Kindergarten students to writing and older Kindergarten students to difficult to spell words. It is easy to model, and fast finisher activities can be added easily. Offer some incentives to motivate students to finish.

Ages	Interaction patterns	Estimated duration	Make it easier by	Make it harder by	Materials
2 – 5	T – S	5 – 10 minutes	Using individual words	Having a non-tracing section where students must write the words without assistance	Tracing worksheets, pencils

Trace And Match

Instructions

1. Ensure students are well drilled in the meaning of the core words.
2. Model how to complete the worksheet.
3. Hand out a tracing worksheet in which the students must trace a word and then match it to an image that represents its meaning.
4. Monitor the students well and help any that are struggling with the activity.
5. Correct errors as they occur.
6. Any common errors that are observed, model them on the board at the end of the activity.
7. Reward students who are trying hard taking and part well.

This is an effective way to expose younger learners to simple writing. Having the students match the word to an image identifies their understanding.

Ages	Interaction patterns	Estimated duration	Make it easier by	Make it harder by	Materials
2 – 5	T – S	5 – 10 minutes	Having them trace only 1 word	Having them trace full sentences	Tracing worksheets, pencils

Colour The Letter

Instructions

1. Ensure the class fully understands the sound required when reading the letter in question.
2. Apply the sound to a real-life thing, an animal or some food.
3. Show the students a worksheet with a balloon letter on it (uncoloured).
4. Demonstrate to the students how to hold a colour and then colour in the letter.
5. Hand out the worksheets and help students keep their colouring within the lines.
6. Give them lots of praise and positive reinforcement.

This activity is aimed at very young learners. It will likely be their first exposure to letters, as such, should be presented in a non-intimidating way.

Ages	Interaction patterns	Estimated duration	Make it easier by	Make it harder by	Materials
2-3	T – S	5 – 10 minutes	Guiding the students hand	Having the students trace the letter too	Worksheets, colours

One Letter Gap Fill

Instructions

1. Introduce the word the students are learning to spell/write.
2. Segment and blend the word a few times to help the students grasp the sounds and form of the word.
3. Show the students a few examples of the word with one letter missing from it.
4. Fill in the missing letter as a whole class.
5. Show the students a worksheet of examples of the word with one letter missing.
6. Demonstrate how to complete the worksheet.
7. Use ICQs to test the students understand what is required of them.
8. Hand out the worksheets and pencils.
9. Help the weak students complete the activity and reward the students who are trying hard.

This is an effective way to expose younger learners to writing and spelling.

Ages	Interaction patterns	Estimated duration	Make it easier by	Make it harder by	Materials
2 – 5	T – S S – T	5 – 10 minutes	Having them trace the letter	Removing more letters	Worksheets pencils

Circle The Word

Instructions

1. Show the students a worksheet with some words on.
2. Demonstrate that when you say a word, they must find it and circle it on the page.
3. Use ICQs to check they understand what is required.
4. Hand out the worksheets.
5. Give the students the pencils.
6. Say aloud the words you want them to circle.
7. Reward the students who are taking part well.

This is a great way to expose learners to the form of some words.

Ages	Interaction patterns	Estimated duration	Make it easier by	Make it harder by	Materials
3 – 5	T – S	5 – 10 minutes	Using only a few words	Having them trace the words	Worksheets and pencils

Listen And Write

Instructions

1. Demonstrate to the students that they are going to listen for a word and then write it on a whiteboard.
2. Practice as a class a few times.
3. Hand out the whiteboards.
4. Hand out the Markers and erasers.
5. Begin the activity, students who write quickly can be awarded points (this is one way of making it a game).
6. Reward students who are taking part well and encourage ones who are not.

This is an effective way to get learners to practice spelling and word formation as a group. Peer-learning also occurs as students can correct themselves from each other's work.

Ages	Interaction patterns	Estimated duration	Make it easier by	Make it harder by	Materials
4 – 5	T – S S – T	5 – 10 minutes	Using short words	Using sentences	White boards, markers and erasers

Walk And Trace

Instructions

1. Split the class into 2 teams.
2. Have the students sit in 2 lines.
3. Split the board in 2.
4. Have words on each side that the students can trace.
5. Show the teams an image that represents one of the words.
6. The first 2 students can go to the board and trace the correlating word.
7. Reward the faster team (writing must still be neat).

This is an effective way to form a healthy competitive environment and encourage students to practice writing in front of their peers. ENSURE STUDENTS ARE SAFE (No running and keep pens by the board in a safe manner).

Ages	Interaction patterns	Estimated duration	Make it easier by	Make it harder by	Materials
4-5	T – S	5 – 10 minutes	Using letters	Using short sentences	Markers, tracing sheets on the board, flashcards

Dot To Dot Letter Exposure

Instructions

1. Create a worksheet with a large dot to dot version of the letter you are teaching on it.
2. Drill the sound with the students.
3. Show the students how to trace over the letter.
4. Hand out the worksheets.
5. Hand out the pencils.
6. Help students who need it by holding the pencil with them.

This is an effective way to first expose students to letters. It is for new writers and is appropriate for all Kindergarten ages

Ages	Interaction patterns	Estimated duration	Make it easier by	Make it harder by	Materials
2 – 5	T – S	5 – 10 minutes	Guiding the students hand	Increasing the number of times the student must trace the letter	Pencils, worksheets

Look And Write

Instructions

1. Make a worksheet of images that the students have learnt to write.
2. Demonstrate to the students that they must look at the picture and write what it is underneath.
3. Use ICQs to check they understand what is required.
4. Hand out the worksheets.
5. Hand out the pencils.
6. Help the students who cannot complete the worksheet on their own.
7. Reward students who are trying hard.

This is an effective way to test students ability remember the form of the words they have learnt. It is not designed for the youngest years in kindergarten.

Ages	Interaction patterns	Estimated duration	Make it easier by	Make it harder by	Materials
4 – 5	T – S	5 – 10 minutes	Having tracing guides under the picture	Having the students write full sentences	Pencils, worksheets

★★My favourite

Free Writing For Kindergarten

Instructions

1. Demonstrate to the students that they are going to have some time to write whatever they want. It can be sentences or just random words.
2. The students are given complete freedom to be creative and come up with whatever they want to
3. Hand out some paper.
4. Hand out some pencils.
5. Encourage the students to write some words, props and flashcards can be used if necessary.
6. Reward students who are trying hard.

This is a great way to give students the opportunity to be creative and use high order thinking skills in writing. Students can present their work once completed.

Ages	Interaction patterns	Estimated duration	Make it easier by	Make it harder by	Materials
4-5	T – S	5 – 10 minutes	Using props and flashcards	Requiring full sentences	Worksheets, pencils, props, flashcards

Listening

A listening activity done well!

Okay, maybe putting the kids to sleep is a bad idea if you want them to learn. Picture this: you have to listen to the least relatable piece of audio you can think of, put it in a foreign language, tell yourself there is no point in listening to it, and see how long you last. When expecting your Kindergarten learners to listen to an audio, give them purpose! Tell them why they are listening to it; give them tasks related to it. AND, make it something interesting to them (Rost & Candlin, 2014).

Listen And Colour

Instructions

1. Show the students some worksheets with images on.
2. Demonstrate to the students that, when you say an image and what colour it should be, they should colour it accordingly.
3. Hand out the worksheets.
4. Hand out the colours.
5. Say the words and what colour they should be.
6. Reward students who are taking part and help the ones who need it.

This is an effective way to check if students understand the sounds of the words they are learning.

Ages	Interaction patterns	Estimated duration	Make it easier by	Make it harder by	Materials
3 – 5	T – S	5 – 10 minutes	Using only 2 words	Using full sentences	Worksheets colours

Listen And Circle

Instructions

1. Show the students some worksheets with numbered selections of images.
2. Demonstrate to the students that when you say "number 1 is a cow", they must circle the cow on line number one.
3. Hand out the materials.
4. Begin the activity.
5. Repeat this process, choosing one of the images from each line until the worksheet is completed.
6. Reward students who are trying hard and help the ones who need it.

This is a great way to expose new learners to listening activities. Students can be concept checked easily, and the meaning behind sounds can be identified.

Ages	Interaction patterns	Estimated duration	Make it easier by	Make it harder by	Materials
3 – 5	T – S	5 – 10 minutes	Using only 2 images per number.	Using many images per number	Worksheets, pencils

Listen And Number

Instructions

1. Show the students some worksheets with images on.
2. Demonstrate to the students that, when you say an image and what number it should be, they should number it accordingly.
3. Hand out the worksheets.
4. Hand out the pencils.
5. Say the words and what number they should be.
6. Reward students who are taking part and help the ones who need it.

This is an effective way to check if students understand the sounds of the words they are learning.

Ages	Interaction patterns	Estimated duration	Make it easier by	Make it harder by	Materials
3 – 5	T – S	5 – 10 minutes	Using only 2 words	Using full sentences	Worksheets colours

Listen And Connect The Letters

Instructions

1. Show the students some worksheets with two rows of letters on them.
2. Demonstrate to the students that, when you make a sound, they must begin to connect the sounds. E.g. you say "d", the students draw a line from go to the "d" letter.
3. ICQ to check understanding.
4. Hand out the worksheets.
5. Hand out the pencils.
6. Say the letters out loud and check that students are doing the activity correctly.
7. Reward students who are taking part and help the ones who need it.

This is an effective way to introduce students to phonics and letter sound recognition.

Ages	Interaction patterns	Estimated duration	Make it easier by	Make it harder by	Materials
4 – 5	T – S	5 – 10 minutes	Using only a few letters	Using many letters	Worksheets, pencils

★★ My favourite

Listen And Act

Instructions

1. Demonstrate to the students that you will say a word and they must produce an action.
2. Stand the students up.
3. Say the first word and do the action with them.
4. Slowly start removing the action cues and have the students do the actions themselves.
5. Reward students who are taking part and help the ones who need it.

This is an effective way to expose students to new language and review old content.

Ages	Interaction patterns	Estimated duration	Make it easier by	Make it harder by	Materials
3 – 5	T – S	5 – 10 minutes	Not removing your action cues	Having the students speak the words back to you	None

Treasure hunt

Instructions

1. Hide some things around the room.
2. Demonstrate to the students that when you say "find a _____", they must look around the room and find that thing.
3. When they find it, they can bring it to you and you can reward them.
4. The whole class can be drilled over every word too.
5. Reward students who are trying hard and help the ones who need it.

This is an effective way to expose students to recognising words and their meanings; it is also useful for drilling.

Ages	Interaction patterns	Estimated duration	Make it easier by	Make it harder by	Materials
3 – 5	T – S S – T	5 – 10 minutes	Saying only 1 word	Having students take on the teacher role	Things to be hidden around the room

Listen And Slap

Instructions

1. Stick some flashcards on the board.
2. Demonstrate to the students that they are going to come up in groups; you are going to say one of the flashcards and they have to race to hit it.
3. Ensure safety is drilled.
4. Bring the students up.
5. Line them up in front of the board.
6. Say the flashcard.
7. Reward the fastest student to get to the card.

This is an effective way to drill students, weaker students can follow suit of the stronger students and still find the right flashcard.

Ages	Interaction patterns	Estimated duration	Make it easier by	Make it harder by	Materials
3 – 5	T – S S – T	5 – 10 minutes	Saying only the flashcard and not a sentence	Having the students say the words when they hit the FC	flashcards

Listen And Trace

Instructions

1. Create some worksheets with some images or letters on.
2. Demonstrate to the students that they must listen and trace the letter or image that you say.
3. Hand out the worksheets.
4. Hand out the pencils.
5. Say the letters or images the students must trace (one by one).
6. Reward students who are participating and encourage ones who are not.

This is an effective to expose students to listening activities and get them involved with recognising sounds and connecting them to the meaning.

Ages	Interaction patterns	Estimated duration	Make it easier by	Make it harder by	Materials
3 – 5	T – S	5 – 10 minutes	Saying 1 word and not a sentence	Saying a full sentence	Pencils, worksheets

Move And Stop

Instructions

1. Students follow directions and then stop when told.
2. Directions can be.

"Jump 5 times" "STOP"
"Fly like a bird" "STOP"

3. Students who stop the slowest can be disqualified, or students who stop the fastest can be given points.

This is an effective way to expose students to listening, you can have students take over the teacher role and give the instructions to their friends.

Ages	Interaction patterns	Estimated duration	Make it easier by	Make it harder by	Materials
3 – 5	T – S	5 – 10 minutes	Saying 1 word and not a sentence	Saying a full sentence/using similes	Maybe flashcards if introducing new words

Section 2 Primary

Primary students vary hugely based on the grade/year. They can be managed and encouraged through good reward systems and proper motivation. However, do not focus too heavily on reward systems – excess use of extrinsic motivation has been shown to diminish students' intrinsic motivation (Hennessey, Moran, Altringer, & Amabile, 2015). Basically, motivate them when you need to, and set high but achievable expectations on them. Make your activities engaging and be excited about them! These students still want to please you (usually), be positive and encourage open communication: trust me, it works.

Speaking

If only it went this well...

Teaching speaking to primary learners is great fun! They can be very competent and if pushed correctly, they learn A LOT! Maximise their opportunities to interact together; student to student interactions are invaluable. Bear in mind, students need to learn cumulatively; start off with simple drilling activities and slowly move the students towards using the language creatively (Hammerly, 1991).

They can self-correct very well if given the chance, so avoid feeding them with answers; elicitation always wins here!

Find Somebody Who

Instructions

1. Write on the board some statements that are phrased like, "find somebody who likes apples, find somebody who likes running, find somebody who is 6 years old".
2. Demonstrate to the students that they need to go to their friends one by one, and find people who answer yes to these questions.
3. They can do this on pieces of paper or premade worksheets.
4. If they are, hand out materials right before they start.
5. Inform the students to begin.
6. Monitor them and reward students who are trying hard.

This is an effective way to have students warm up for a lesson and get comfortable speaking together.

Ages	Interaction patterns	Estimated duration	Make it easier by	Make it harder by	Materials
5 – 11	T – S S – S S – T	5 – 10 minutes	Using simple statements like "likes apples"	Using complex statements	Paper, pencils

Pair Work Drill

Instructions

1. Expose the language to be drilled to the students.
2. Show them a simple 2 way conversation they can have using it.
3. Model the conversation at the front of the class.
4. Put the students into pairs and give them a model of the conversation on the board.
5. Tell the students to start the activity.
6. Listen for errors, correct them where necessary.
7. Reward students who are taking part and trying hard.

This is an effective way to have students drill and practice language together.

Ages	Interaction patterns	Estimated duration	Make it easier by	Make it harder by	Materials
5 – 11	T – S S – S	5 – 10 minutes	Using simple verbs "like"	Using complex verbs "guess"	board marker

Rock Paper Scissors Review

Instructions

1. Hand out some worksheets with imagery resembling the content you want to review.
2. Demonstrate to the students that they will work in pairs and play rock paper scissors with each other; the winner can make a sentence using one of the images.
3. Once an image has been used, they can tick it off
4. The student who ticks off the images first is the winner.
5. Reward them and rearrange the pairs for another game.

This is a great way to get students to review a topic and practice communication with their peers. It is fun and engaging. Students regularly request this game but do not overdo it.

Ages	Interaction patterns	Estimated duration	Make it easier by	Make it harder by	Materials
5 – 11	T – S S – S	5 – 15 minutes	Requiring students to say only 1 word	Requiring students to make full sentences	Worksheets, pencils

Surveys

Instructions

1. Create a survey table related to the topic.
2. Demonstrate to the students that they will be walking around the room and asking their peers the questions in their survey table to get answers.
3. As they get answers they must fill in the spaces on the survey table.
4. Fast finishers can make sentences using the information they have gathered.
5. At the end of the activity, you can do a whole class summary of what was discovered.

This is a great way to get students to practice language communicatively on a large scale. It encourages peer to peer learning and practices fluency as well.

Ages	Interaction patterns	Estimated duration	Make it easier by	Make it harder by	Materials
5 – 11	S – S T – S	5 – 20 minutes	Providing imagery & sentence starters	Having students answer complex open questions	Worksheets, pencils

Questionnaire

Instructions

1. Show the students an example of a questionnaire that is related to the content they have been learning.
2. Demonstrate to them how to ask people the questions and fill them in.
3. Either have the students create their own questionnaires or give them templates that you have created.
4. Ask the students to begin taking the questionnaires, using the questions, as a tool to practice their speaking skills.
5. Fast finishers can create a text based on their results.

This is an effective way to get students to review learning and be creative with language at the same time.

Ages	Interaction patterns	Estimated duration	Make it easier by	Make it harder by	Materials
5 – 11	T – S S – S	10 – 20 minutes	Giving the students templates	Having the students create the questionnaires	Template questionnaires, pencils

★★ My favourite

Board Games

Instructions

1. Use a board game template and draw or insert images on the spaces.
2. Make sure the images are related to the content students are learning/reviewing.
3. Students can play the board games in pairs, teams or you can play it on the chalk board as a class.
4. As students play, they have to ask and answer questions related to the pictures.
5. As students win the board game, you can give them little rewards.
6. Motivate and help students who need it.

This is a great way to get students to review and/or be creative with content. It can be adapted to incorporate writing short sentences.

Ages	Interaction patterns	Estimated duration	Make it easier by	Make it harder by	Materials
5 – 11	T – S S – S	10 – 20 minutes	Having students simply say the word correlating with the image	Having the students create their own board games	Board game templates, pencils, dice, counters

Big Dice Drill

Instructions

1. Write numbers 1 to 6 on the board.
2. Next to each number, add a phrase, image or word related to the lesson content.
3. Demonstrate to the students that when you throw the dice, they have to race to say the sentence on the board that corresponds with the number on the dice.
4. You can put the students in teams to make it competitive.
5. You can let students throw the dice for you.

This is a great warm up activity and can be used to drill language in a fun and competitive way.

Ages	Interaction patterns	Estimated duration	Make it easier by	Make it harder by	Materials
5 – 11	T – S S – S	5 – 10 minutes	Having students say one word	Having students say full sentences	A big dice

Snowball Fight

Instructions

1. Hand out some paper to students.
2. Have them all write a question on the paper.
3. Once written, they can put away their pencils.
4. Have them scrunch up the paper into balls.
5. Demonstrate to them that it is okay to throw them at each other "safely".
6. Get them to pick up one each.
7. They can open the paper up and read aloud the question, and then answer it.

This is a fun way to get students to review content or warm-up for a lesson. You can give out paper that already has questions on it to tailor the responses

Ages	Interaction patterns	Estimated duration	Make it easier by	Make it harder by	Materials
5 – 11	T – S S – S	5 – 10 minutes	Having an image on the paper and students only need to say the word	Having students write down each other's answers	Paper, pencils

Tell 5 Friends

Instructions

1. This is usually an end of lesson activity but could be used at any time with any topic.
2. Write on the board "tell 5 friends about what you learnt".
3. Demonstrate to the students that they will stand up, walk around the room, and tell 5 of their friends about what they learnt.
4. You can make the phrase more specific to read something like, "tell 5 friends the animals we talked about".
5. Monitor the students and reward the ones who are trying hard.

This is great way to review topics and build students fluency.

Ages	Interaction Patterns	Estimated duration	Make it easier by	Make it harder by	Materials
5 – 11	T – S S – S	5 minutes	Making the instruction very specific	Making the instruction open	A marker

Ladder Climb

Instructions

1. Create a worksheet that has a ladder on it.
2. On each rung of the ladder should be an image or word that you are teaching.
3. Students start at the bottom of their ladders and play rock paper scissors.
4. The winner can climb one rung on the worksheet but must make a sentence using the image or word that is inside the rung of ladder that they land on.
5. They repeat this process till one of them reaches the top (they are the winner).
6. You can reward the winners to motivate the students to keep playing.

This is a great productive activity where students get to create sentences.

Ages	Interaction patterns	Estimated duration	Make it easier by	Make it harder by	Materials
5 – 11	T – S S – S	5 – 20 minutes	Having the students simply say one word	Having the students ask questions rather than make statements	Ladder worksheets. You can give the students counters too.

Reading

This kid is at it again!

By primary age, students are usually gaining some competence at reading. This is not always the case though. There will be largely differing levels within your class. As with all lessons, you should differentiate your activities (make them suitable for different levels of students). Giving students free choice and some library time can be effective (if you have that option). Your students should want to read what you give them: or very little learning will occur (Gallagher, 2009). Help the ones who need it using segmenting and blending (see page 5).

Read And Answer

Instructions

1. Create a text relevant to the students and the learning goals.
2. Make some questions based on the text.
3. Give the students the text and the questions.
4. They must read it and answer the questions.
5. Give assistance to students who need it.

This is an example of a reading comprehension activity. The text and the questions can be tailored to the age and ability of the group. The text can also be made meaningful and relevant to the students.

Ages	Interaction Patterns	Estimated duration	Make it easier by	Make it harder by	Materials
5 – 11	T – S	5 – 20 minutes	Having the students answer simple questions	Having the students create questions themselves	Text and questions worksheet. pencils

★★ My favourite

Running Dictation

Instructions

1. Put some pieces of text up on the wall.
2. Put students in pairs.
3. Give them a piece of the text with words missing.
4. One student goes to the text on the wall and reads a part of it.
5. They go back to their partner and dictate what they have read.
6. The partner uses this information to fill in the missing words.

This is an effective way to get students to work collaboratively in a reading activity. They can take turns to read the text and you can make it competitive by having the class race (safely).

Ages	Interaction Patterns	Estimated duration	Make it easier by	Make it harder by	Materials
5 – 11	T – S S – S	5 – 20 minutes	Have 1 word missing	Have full sentences missing and/or the whole text	Worksheets, pencils, text for the walls

Face Away Reading

Instructions

1. Create a piece of text that is relevant and meaningful to the students and the topic.
2. Make two versions of this text, each with different sentences blanked out.
3. Students sit facing away from each other and take turns reading out the text till they reach a gap.
4. When they reach a gap, the other student continues to read and the first student fills the gap.
5. The students repeat this till the gaps are all filled.

This is a great way to get students comfortable with reading aloud to their peers.

Ages	Interaction Patterns	Estimated duration	Make it easier by	Make it harder by	Materials
5 – 11	T – S S – S	5 – 20 minutes	Have 1 word missing	Have full sentences missing and/or the whole text	Original text, student versions with blank outs, pencils

Whole Text Gap fill

Instructions

1. Create a piece of text that is relevant and meaningful to the students and the topic.
2. Blank out a series of words in the text.
3. Give students the text, they need to try to figure out what words should go in the blanked out spaces.
4. You can provide a complete version of the text up on the board for the students to check their answers against.

This is an effective way to get students to be creative, and/or review content they have covered so far.

Ages	Interaction patterns	Estimated duration	Make it easier by	Make it harder by	Materials
5 – 11	T – S S – S	5 – 20 minutes	Providing a word key	Have full sentences missing and/or the whole text	Original text, student versions with blank outs, pencils

1 Minute Skim

Instructions

1. Create a piece of text that is relevant and meaningful to the students and the topic.
2. Give the students the piece of text.
3. Tell them they have 1 minute to skim read it and get an idea of what it is about.
4. Once 1 minute is up they must turn over their paper.
5. You then ask them key questions to elicit what they have learnt.
6. The class can then have a discussion about what they learnt.
7. You can reward the students who are trying hard.

This is an effective way to expose students to/get students to practice skim reading. This is a skill that they can use in a range of different situations.

Ages	Interaction patterns	Estimated duration	Make it easier by	Make it harder by	Materials
5 – 11	T – S S – S	5 – 10 minutes	Using a very short text	Using a long text	Pieces of text for students

Scanning

Instructions

1. Create a piece of text that is relevant and meaningful to the students and the topic.
2. Provide some questions up on the board and read them as a class.
3. Hand out the texts and the students can race to see who is able to scan the text the fastest and answer all of the questions.
4. You can have the faster students write their own questions about the text so slower ones have time to finish.

This is an effective way to expose students to the skill scanning. This is an attribute they can use in a range of different situations.

Ages	Interaction patterns	Estimated duration	Make it easier by	Make it harder by	Materials
5 – 11	T – S S – S	5 – 20 minutes	Using a very short text	Using a long text with complex phrasing	Piece of text, questions, pencils

Surveying

Instructions

1. Give the students a few pieces of text that have opinions and facts on.
2. Tell the students they will be surveying the text.
3. Explain that this means they will look over it generally and decide if it is worth reading more into; they may well pick out some key bits of information they notice.
4. You can even have them rank order the pieces of text in regards to a certain topic.
5. This can be done in groups and they can debate which pieces of text are more valuable.

This is an effective way to expose students to the skill surveying. It is not as simple as some of the other reading activities but can be appropriate with stronger classes.

Ages	Interaction patterns	Estimated duration	Make it easier by	Make it harder by	Materials
9 - 11	T – S S – S	5 – 20 minutes	Using short texts	Using long texts with complex words and phrasing	Pieces of text, pencils

Speed Read

Instructions

1. Create a piece of text that is relevant and meaningful to the students and the topic.
2. Blow it up and put it on the board (or write it up on the board).
3. Have the students read one word each and see how well they can keep the flow of the text.
4. You can set targets for the students "if you can read the first line without mistake or hesitation, you can win _____".
5. This can be used as a warmer in a reading lesson or to introduce a text

This is an effective way to make reading a bit more fun for students.

Ages	Interaction patterns	Estimated duration	Make it easier by	Make it harder by	Materials
5 - 11	T – S S – S	5 – 10 minutes	Using short texts	Using long texts with complex words and phrasing	Blown up piece of text, markers

Read And Summarise

Instructions

1. Create a piece of text that is relevant and meaningful to the students and the topic.
2. Hand out copies to the students and tell them they have X amount of time to read it and remember as much as they can.
3. Collect the texts once the time is up.
4. Students can then have a short period of time to summarise what the text was about.
5. They can do this in pairs, groups or individually.

This is an effective way to have students read a text, and then try to understand it on a deeper level.

Ages	Interaction patterns	Estimated duration	Make it easier by	Make it harder by	Materials
7 – 11	T – S S – S	5 – 15 minutes	Using short texts	Using long texts with complex words and phrasing	Pieces of text, paper to summarise on, pencils

Team Choral Reading

Instructions

1. Create a piece of text that is relevant and meaningful to the students and the topic.
2. Put the class into two teams.
3. Either, give the students each a copy of the text or blow it up/write it on the board.
4. Teams can take turns to read a paragraph or sentence.
5. Whichever team reads more clearly and in unison can receive rewards.
6. After each reading, you can question the teams who were listening and reward them for answering questions correctly.

This is an effective way to get all of the students to read in front of their peers. It can help students with more language barriers with intonation and pronunciation.

Ages	Interaction patterns	Estimated duration	Make it easier by	Make it harder by	Materials
5 - 11	T – S S – S	5 – 15 minutes	Using short texts	Using long texts with complex words and phrasing.	Pieces of text, pencils

Writing

Darts 2.0 – It was bad both times

Students in different years/grade in primary schools have very different needs when it comes to writing (Palmer, 2010). Still, the same activities are often applicable. Slight alterations make the same activity new, engaging and fun for a whole different year group. It is up to you to know your learners and how to approach writing lessons with them. Typically, giving them the choice to write about what they want is an effective way; this is engaging and keeps them going through the tough bits.

IMPROVE YOUR PRACTICE TODAY

Write A Short Story

Instructions

1. Give the students some examples of stories, highlight to them that all stories must have a beginning, middle, and an end.
2. Let the students create a short plan of what will happen at each of these stages.
3. Let the students begin to write their story; it is wise to give them time limits to complete each section.
4. Help students who need it.
5. Let students read each other's stories and comment on what they liked best.

This is a great way to practice language, creative writing and story structures.

Ages	Interaction patterns	Estimated duration	Make it easier by	Make it harder by	Materials
7 – 11	T – S S – S	10 – 30 minutes	Providing a series of images for them to write about	Having them include some difficult new words	Paper, pencils

★★ My favourite

Finish the story

Instructions

1. Show the students the beginning and middle of a story.
2. Ask them to work in groups to figure out what they think might happen next.
3. Provide them with some paper and pencils, and inform them that they are going to write their own ending to the story.
4. You can give them a short period of time in which they need to plan what they are writing.
5. Upon completion, you can have them pass their stories around and read each other's endings. They can leave a short comment on what they liked best

This is an effective way to get students to be creative in their writing. It also makes the writing process a little easier as they have a framework to write off (the story)

Ages	Interaction patterns	Estimated duration	Make it easier by	Make it harder by	Materials
6 – 11	T – S S – S	10 – 40 minutes	Providing a story ending template or sentence starters	Giving little assistance	Paper, pencils, storybook

Add The Adjectives/Adverbs

Instructions

1. Find or create a piece of text that you know will be significant to the students.
2. Remove all of the adjectives in the story.
3. Elicit a range of adjectives from the students as a warm-up.
4. Explain to them that they will be getting the piece of text you made; they have to add the adjectives.
5. Tell them to be as creative as possible.
6. Once completed, students can take turns to read their versions of the text to the class.

This is an effective way to practice and review writing structures and adjective use. It is an activity that can be used in the lead up to students writing their own pieces of text on a topic.

Ages	Interaction patterns	Estimated duration	Make it easier by	Make it harder by	Materials
6 – 11	T – S S – S	10 – 20 minutes	Give a long list of adjective suggestions	Use a longer piece of text	Pieces of text, pencils

Write An Opinion Piece

Instructions

1. Inform students they will be writing an opinion piece
2. Have students work in groups or individually to generate ideas around a relevant topic.
3. Have students work individually to begin focusing their ideas.
4. Have students begin to organise their ideas.
5. Have students write their opinion pieces.
6. Students can peer review and read each other's work.
7. Go and research "OREO Writing", there is a plethora of great resources for this.

This is an effective way to get students to write creatively and practice their writing skills. It can be topic related and/or freer.

Ages	Interaction patterns	Estimated duration	Make it easier by	Make it harder by	Materials
6 – 11	T – S S – S	10 – 60 minutes	Provide story templates and sentence starters	Have a list of complex abstract words students must use	paper, pencils

Free Writing For Primary

Instructions

1. Demonstrate to the students that they are going to have some time to write whatever they want. It should be sentences and you can make it topic related.
2. The students are given freedom to be creative and come up with ideas on what they want to write.
3. Hand out some paper.
4. Hand out some pencils.
5. Encourage the students to write whatever they want to on the topic, creativity should flow and they should know that they will not be graded on mistakes.
6. Reward students who are trying hard.

This is a great way to give students the opportunity to be creative and use high order thinking skills in writing. Students can present their work once completed.

Ages	Interaction patterns	Estimated duration	Make it easier by	Make it harder by	Materials
6 – 11	T – S	10 – 20 minutes	Providing sentence starters	Giving no assistance	paper, pencils, props, flashcards

One Sentence Each

Instructions

1. Put the students into groups.
2. Each group can have a sheet of paper and a pencil.
3. Students take turns to write a sentence about a topic you have presented them with.
4. They write this at the top of the paper, then fold it down so their sentence is hidden.
5. The group can do this until the paper is full. Once completed, they can read their work to the class.

This is a great way to get students to practice using conjunctions in a creative way.

Ages	Interaction patterns	Estimated duration	Make it easier by	Make it harder by	Materials
6 – 11	T – S S – S	10 – 20 minutes	Providing sentence starters	Giving complex words they must each use	paper, pencils

Write A Letter (formal or informal)

Instructions

1. Show the students some letters; you can use age-appropriate ones you have received to make them authentic.
2. Teach them how to lay out a letter.
3. Have the students think about who they might write to.
4. Have students work individually to begin focusing their ideas.
5. Have students begin to organise their ideas.
6. Have students write their letters.
7. Students can peer review and read each other's work.

This is an effective way to teach students how to write a letter and have it relevant to them.

Ages	Interaction patterns	Estimated duration	Make it easier by	Make it harder by	Materials
6 – 11	T – S S – S	10 – 20 minutes	Providing a letter template	Giving complex words they must each use	paper, pencils, letter templates

Opposites

Instructions

1. Provide the students with a list of statements, paragraphs or words.
2. The students must go through the list and rewrite the statement, paragraph or word so that it has the opposite meaning (for antonyms).
3. You can have the students reword the sentences to have the same meaning but using different words (for synonyms).
4. Students can do this in pairs or groups if necessary.
5. Once completed, students can compare their answers.

This is an effective way to get students to practice writing and expose them to synonyms and antonyms.

Ages	Interaction patterns	Estimated duration	Make it easier by	Make it harder by	Materials
6 – 11	T – S S – S	10 – 20 minutes	Using only 1 word and providing a list of potential words to choose from	Using paragraphs	paper, pencils, worksheets

Condensation

Instructions

1. Explain to the students that they will be writing a short story. 3 paragraphs should be fine.
2. Once completed, have the students condense this into 3 sentences.
3. Once completed, have the students condense these into 3 words.
4. You can take this a step further and have them decide on 1 word.

This is a fun way to get students to practice writing creatively. You can have them peer-assess and correct each other's grammar/provide recommendations to each other.

Ages	Interaction patterns	Estimated duration	Make it easier by	Make it harder by	Materials
8 – 11	T – S S – S	20 – 30 minutes	Giving story examples	Having students write more than 3 paragraphs or giving them complicated words they must use	Story templates, pencils, paper

Poetry and Rhyming

Instructions

1. Give the students some examples of poems and rhymes.
2. Demonstrate to them how to write one.
3. Have the students generate ideas for their poems.
4. Have the students begin to focus on these ideas.
5. Have the students organise these ideas so as to structure their poems.
6. They can then write their own poems and rhymes.
7. Allow the students to peer evaluate.

This is an effective way to get students to practice writing creatively and to understand rhymes and poetry.

Ages	Interaction patterns	Estimated duration	Make it easier by	Make it harder by	Materials
6 – 11	T – S S – S	10 – 30 minutes	Providing words that rhyme for them	Having the students write about a difficult concept	paper, pencils, worksheets

Listening

Looks like we did it again, it was probably that audio track from the textbook that was provided… They almost never work. Be creative with your lessons; write a script and some questions yourself, this way the audio tracks are more relatable for your students. You can read it yourself; maybe you have a top student who can read it for you: double win.

Remember to set your students' expectations, let them know how long things will take and what they will be doing. Not knowing how long something will take increases stress and frustration: this is well seen in people waiting at train stations, if there is no guide of how long till the train arrives; we experience higher levels of stress and frustration than if we have a timer telling us how long to wait (Larson, Larson, & Katz, 1991). Bear this in mind when teaching your students, keep them in the loop.

Listen And Answer

Instructions

1. Provide the students with a list of questions relevant to an audio or text that you will read.
2. Give the students an example of how to answer the question based on the listening.
3. Read the questions with the students.
4. Read the text and have the students listen and answer the questions you provided.
5. The students can peer assess; have them swap sheets, and then elicit the correct answers from the class.

This is an effective way to get students to practice listening for specific pieces of information; you can have strong students read the text out.

Ages	Interaction Patterns	Estimated duration	Make it easier by	Make it harder by	Materials
6 – 11	T – S S – S	10 minutes	Reading slowly or putting emphasis on important parts of the text	Having students read it out or reading faster	Questions worksheets, pencils

Listen And Sort

Instructions

1. Give the students some genres, topics or concepts. These can be as simple as "good" and "bad" or more complicated such as "romance" and "action".
2. You can either read a list of words for them to sort into genres, or a series of short poems/stories.
3. Upon completion of the activity, the students can have group discussions or peer assess each other's decisions.
4. This is a good activity that can be used as a warmer or as concept checks.

This is an effective way to get students to practice listening for meaning. Students can do this individually or in pairs/groups.

Ages	Interaction patterns	Estimated duration	Make it easier by	Make it harder by	Materials
6 – 11	T – S S – S	10 minutes	Using only 1 word at a time	Using difficult concepts and having students listen to short stories instead of words	Sorting sheets, pencils.

★★ My favourite

Listen For Gist Group Poster

Instructions

1. Prepare a relevant and meaningful piece of listening for the students.
2. Inform the students that they will listen to the audio, and after they have listened, they will work in groups to create a poster.
3. The posters will be made to represent everything the students can remember from the audio. They can use whatever poster format they want or that you set them.
4. Play the audio; let the students make the posters.
5. Once completed, pencils are to be put down and they can take turns to do a presentation, you can have them grade each other.

This is an effective way to get students to practice listening for gist and produce a creative group project.

Ages	Interaction patterns	Estimated duration	Make it easier by	Make it harder by	Materials
6 – 11	T – S S – S	10 – 30 minutes	Giving visual cues to act as reminders for regarding the audio	Using a long and complicated audio	Posters, pencils, maybe colours.

Listen And Discuss

Instructions

1. Prepare a relevant and meaningful piece of listening for the students.
2. Inform the students that they will listen to the audio, and after they have listened, they are going to formulate opinions on what was said.
3. They can begin by deciding whether they like or dislike it; they then can decide why.
4. You can have students make small mind maps to help them formulate their ideas/opinions.
5. After this, students can have a group or class discussion about their ideas and opinions regarding the audio.

This is an effective way to get students to practice listening to an audio and analysing their thoughts on it. It also gives them a chance to critique.

Ages	Interaction patterns	Estimated duration	Make it easier by	Make it harder by	Materials
7 – 11	T – S S – S	10 – 30 minutes	Modelling your opinion and thoughts on the audio first	Using a complex issue in the audio	Mind maps, pencils

Listen And Order

Instructions

1. Prepare a relevant and meaningful piece of listening for the students.
2. From the audio, create a text.
3. Split the text up into a series of sentences.
4. Have the students listen to the audio and order the sentences.
5. You may need to play the audio 2 or 3 times.
6. Once completed, have the students compare orders to see if they got it right.
7. Students who tried hard can be rewarded.

This is an effective way to get students to practice listening and perhaps working in groups or pairs.

Ages	Interaction patterns	Estimated duration	Make it easier by	Make it harder by	Materials
7 – 11	T – S S – S	10 – 30 minutes	Using images and a series of word instead of a whole audio text	Using a complex audio file with some words they do not know	Texts broken up into sentences

Who Said It?

Instructions

1. Students are given some information about 4 different people.
2. The information could be simple, what they like, where they are from etc.
3. Students can listen to four different texts and try to figure out who said each one.
4. You can play them one by one and students can discuss in groups who they think said it.
5. You can incentivise students to work in teams to get all 4 correct for a prize.
6. If you have no audio, you can read a text yourself. You can also create the text yourself to keep it interesting to the students.

This is an effective way to get students to practice listening in groups. It can be competitive and test their ability to pick up on keywords.

Ages	Interaction patterns	Estimated duration	Make it easier by	Make it harder by	Materials
7 – 11	T – S S – S	10 – 15 minutes	Putting emphasis on keywords that are said	Using complicated texts that contain many new words	Paper with information about 4 different people

Descriptive Selection

Instructions

1. Give the students a series of images and/or pictures.
2. You can begin to describe them.
3. As you describe them, students must try to figure out which picture you are describing.
4. E.g. "It is big, it is red" (fire truck picture).
5. Students can either race to see who can figure it out first, or they can number the images based on the order you read the descriptions.
6. Students can peer grade each other's work.

This is an effective way to get students to practice listening in groups. It can be competitive and test their ability to pick up on keywords.

Ages	Interaction patterns	Estimated duration	Make it easier by	Make it harder by	Materials
7 – 11	T – S S – S	10 – 15 minutes	Using simple and obvious descriptions	Using complex and abstract descriptions	Worksheets, pencils

Listen And Create

Instructions

1. Tell the students they are going to hear an audio.
2. Once the audio has been played, they are going to create some questions related to the audio.
3. You can play the audio 2 or 3 times for them.
4. Once they have created the questions, they can swap paper with their peers and see if they can answer the questions their peers have created.
5. Upon completion, they swap back and mark each other's work.

This is an effective way to get students to practice listening closely and carefully. It requires high order thinking skills and creativity.

Ages	Interaction patterns	Estimated duration	Make it easier by	Make it harder by	Materials
7 – 11	T – S S – S	20 – 30 minutes	Using a simple text	Using a longer and more complicated text	Paper, pencils

Dictogloss

Instructions

1. Play the students an audio or read them a text you prepared.
2. Tell the students they are going to listen again; after this attempt, they will be trying to rewrite what was said.
3. During this listening, allow the students to note down keywords.
4. Students then try to reconstruct the text from the keywords they have noted down.
5. This can be done individually or in pairs/groups.
6. Once completed, the students can be given the original text to check how well they have managed to rewrite the text.

This is an effective way to get students to train their memory and listen very carefully. It also allows them to figure out which words are important when listening to people.

Ages	Interaction patterns	Estimated duration	Make it easier by	Make it harder by	Materials
9 – 11	T – S S – S	10 – 30 minutes	Using a simple text	Using a longer and more complicated text	Paper, pencils

Listen And Draw

Instructions

1. Students listen to some drawing instructions e.g.
"Draw a circle in the middle of the page"
"Draw a star to the left of the circle"
"Draw a square under the star"
2. They need to follow the instructions and draw as best they can based on them.
3. Upon completion the students can check their work against one you have done earlier.

This is an effective way to check students know some key words; it is also an effective way for them to review directions and propositions of place.

Ages	Interaction patterns	Estimated duration	Make it easier by	Make it harder by	Materials
6 – 11	T – S S – S	5 - 10 minutes	Having them draw the images next to numbers	Using a longer and more complicated text	Paper, pencils

What now?

Using these activities, you can start to create your own activity bank. How you set it up and what you consider to be valuable is up to you. Mixing up the activities you find in here and being creative with them is a reasonable place to start. Teachers should be creative and adaptive; let's be teachers who can help students overcome any problems they encounter in productive and positive ways.

Personal Development

Personal development is a key part of a teacher's job. The old adage "The best teachers never stop learning" is still around for a reason. Take the ideas from this book, and develop them in your own ways.

There are also a range of courses in EFL education available on the site; these are developmental for anybody who works with EAL, ESL and EFL students. These courses, not only teach you in-depth and applicable knowledge, they are also powerful on your professional resume.

Though pricing is not high, there are options for scholarships to study; these are for people who cannot afford to pay for their fees but demonstrate a real passion and thirst to improve and develop their teaching practice. Teachers who are continuously reflective, and deeply understand the concept of being a lifelong learner are integral to the improvement of educational systems worldwide. I would point anybody looking to push themselves further to look at University Of The People's Master's in Education.

Safety

The activities mentioned in this book should all be used in a safe manner; ensuring student safety is of the utmost importance to a teacher. Before considering implementing anything suggested, double-check the layout of the classroom and be sure that students can take part in the activity without risk. If the classroom has hard floors or lots of tables and chairs, activities with running or a lot of moving around are not appropriate, and more stationary activities could be applied.

Bonus Activities

This is an example of Gregory Macur's activity bank minus the activities that have been broken down into simple instructions throughout this book. If some of the names seem interesting to you, do some further research into what the activity constitutes.

Warmers	Practice activities	Productive activities
Finish the thought	Charades	Debate
I went to the market	Board Race	Make an advert
Simon Says	Find your other half	Interviews
Hangman	Pictionary	Create a comic
Sing a Song	Speed gap fill	Mingle
Swap Seats	Match the sets	Create a character
Last Letter First	Slow and fast speech	Write a biography
		Write an autobiography
		Create a speech

Acronyms & Definitions

CCQ – Concept checking question. Used to check students' understanding of the meaning behind a word or phrase. Simple yes or no questions are advised.

ICQ – Instruction checking question. Used to check students' understanding of the instructions they have been given. Simple yes or no questions are advised.

Lexis – another way of saying vocabulary.

EFL – English Foreign Language.

TEFL – Teaching English as a Foreign Language.

ESL – English Second Language.

EAL – English as an Additional Language.

Peer to Peer – in our context, this means "student to student".

Differentiation – changing activities so as to meet the needs of all students.

When I came up with the idea of this book, I made a quick sketch on my phone in notes. I came up with the basic structure of how I would present each activity page. I began to build on that idea.

People who write things down are over 40% more likely to do them (Gardner & Albee, 2015): so right now, picture what it is you want to do, put this book down, and go write it down.

Good luck ☺

Bibliography

Altinel, Z. (2006). Student misbehavior in EFL classes: teachers' and students' perspectives. *Cukurova University*.

Awaluddin, A. (2013). Techniques in presenting vocabulary to young EFL learners. *Journal of English and Education*, 11-20.

Balser, T. J., Grabau, A. A., Kniess, D., & Page, L. A. (2017). Collaboration and communication. *New directions for institutional research*, 65-79.

British Council. (n.d.). *Backchaining*. Retrieved 4 13, 22, from teachingenglish: https://www.teachingenglish.org.uk/article/backchaining

Brown, S. (2018). Task-Based Approach to Listening. *The TESOL encyclopedia of English language teaching*, 1-6.

Dornyei, Z., & Kubanyiova, M. (2014). *Motivating learners, motivating teachers: Building vision in the language classroom*. Cambridge: Cambridge University Press (CUP).

Double, K. S., McGrane, J. A., & Hopfenbeck, T. N. (2020). The impact of peer assessment on academic performance: A meta-analysis of control group studies. *Educational Psychology Review*, 481-509.

Dumančić, D. (2018). Investigating boredom among EFL teachers. *ExELL (Explorations in English Language and Linguistics)*, 57-80.

Gallagher, K. (2009). *Readicide: How schools are killing reading and what you can do about it*. Portland: Stenhouse Publishers.

Galton, M., & Williamson, J. (2003). *Group work in the primary classroom*. Routledge.

Gao, X. A. (2010). *Strategic language learning: The roles of agency and context*. Bristol: Multilingual Matters.

Gardner, S., & Albee, D. (2015). Study focuses on strategies for achieving goals, resolutions. *Press Releases*, 266.

Hammerly, H. (1991). *Fluency and Accuracy: Toward Balance in Language Teaching and Learning*. Clevedon: Multilingual Matters Ltd.

Harmer, J. (2008). How to teach English. *ELT journal*, 313-316.

Hennessey, B., Moran, S., Altringer, B., & Amabile, T. M. (2015). Extrinsic and intrinsic motivation. *Wiley encyclopedia of management*, 1-4.

Hyland, K. (2019). *Second language writing*. Cambridge: Cambridge university press.

Larson, R. C., Larson, B. M., & Katz, K. L. (1991). Prescription for waiting–in line blues: Entertain, enlighten and engage. *Sloan Management review*, 44-55.

Macur, G. (2020). The Purpose Of Education. *Int. J. of Adv. Res*, 983-985.

Macur, G. M. (2020). A critical evaluation of an EAL intervention put in place to prepare weaker EAL students for the motivation and language required at the primary stage recommendations for improvement are provided. *International Journal of Advanced Research*, 684-694.

Maftoon, P., & Sarem, S. N. (2015). A critical look at the presentation, practice, production (ppp) approach: challenges and promises for ELT. *Broad Research in Artificial Intelligence and Neuroscience*, 31-36.

Meyers, E. S. (1973). *The Kindergarten Teacher's Handbook.* Los Angeles: Gramercy Press.

Palmer, S. (2010). *How to Teach Writing Across the Curriculum: Ages 6-8.* United Kingdom: Routledge.

Pang, E. S., Bernhardt, E. B., & Kamil, M. L. (2003). *Teaching reading (Vol. 6).* Brussels: International Academy of Education.

Rahimi, A., & Dastjerdi, H. V. (2012). Impact of immediate and delayed error correction on EFL learners' oral production. *Mediterranean Journal of Social Sciences*, 45-45.

Reid, G. (2007). *Motivating learners in the classroom: Ideas and strategies.* Sage.

Richards, J. C., & Rodgers, T. S. (2014). *Approaches and methods in language teaching.* Cambridge : Cambridge university press.

Rost, M., & Candlin, C. N. (2014). *Listening in language learning.* Routledge.

Saricoban, A. (2002). Reading strategies of successful readers through the three phase approach. *The Reading Matrix.*

© 2022 Gregory Macur

All rights reserved. This book or any portion thereof may not be reproduced or used in any manner whatsoever without the express written permission of the writer. Any attempt to do so will result in legal consequences.

www.ingramcontent.com/pod-product-compliance
Lightning Source LLC
Chambersburg PA
CBHW051656040426
42446CB00009B/1159